Other Books by Daniel Hoffman

Broken Laws
Striking the Stones
The City of Satisfactions
A Little Geste
An Armada of Thirty Whales

Poe Poe Poe Poe Poe Poe Poe
Barbarous Knowledge
Form and Fable in American Fiction
The Poetry of Stephen Crane
Paul Bunyan, Last of the Frontier Demigods

As Editor:
American Poetry and Poetics
The Red Badge of Courage and Other Tales

The Center of Attention

The
Center of Attention

POEMS BY

Daniel Hoffman

Random House   *New York*

Library of Congress Cataloging in Publication Data
Hoffman, Daniel, 1923—
The center of attention; poems.

I. Title.
PS3515.02416C4   811'.5'4   73–15651
ISBN 0–394–48951–9

Manufactured in the United States of America
9 8 7 6 5 4 3 2
First Edition

Acknowledgments

Thanks to the Ingram Merrill Foundation for a grant in 1971–72, and to the University of Pennsylvania for a leave, during which many of the poems in this book were written. 'Dogfish' is reprinted from *The New Yorker*; 'Comanches,' 'Door,' 'An Old Photo in an Old Life,' 'Path,' 'The Poem,' and 'Shell' first appeared in *Poetry*. Other poems are reprinted by courtesy of *American Poetry Review*, *American Review*, *American Scholar*, *Centennial Review*, *Columbia Forum*, *Denver Quarterly*, *Hearse*, *Hudson Review*, *Humanist*, *The Nation*, *New Republic*, *Pembroke Magazine*, *Pennsylvania Gazette*, *Pennsylvania Review*, *Rain*, *Shenandoah*, and *Southern Review*.

Lizzie: Yours

Contents

I

II

I

After God

'The Jews have a Fancy, that when our Almighty
Creator befpangled the Heavens with the *Stars of
Night*, He left a Space near the Northern Pole,
unfinifhed and unfurnifhed, that if any *After-God*
fhould lay claim to Deity, a challenge to fill up that
fpace might Eternally confute it.'

—*Cotton Mather*

Who keeps His ceaselessly attentive eye
Upon the flight and fall
Of each Polaris through the wide feast-hall
Of the sky,
So like the life of man from dark
To dark in a little space,

Who in this bowling alley spins
Balls of light
At the back of the North Wind
Careening as their plastic skins
Mirror widdershins
Our sponsored images,

Who flings bright strands of platinum hair
And unpointed needles wandering
Through the frozen stratosphere
In a confusion
Of jagged rays
Until True North is lost,

Who deafens the Aurora Borealis
With climbing fire,
Who spurts with the desire
That blazes and subsides in ashen
Droppings of contagion
After the whirlwind,

3

Him we beseech
As adepts who would scan and preach
The Providences of His will.
Be done, send us a sign
That we may read
By the shrivelled light of our gelded sun

The sentence of our sufferings.
His blood flames now
Against the Northern sky.
He walks among us, visible.
The next dawn brings
A vacant hour that sacrifice can fill.

Dark of the Moon

Squinting through smoked glass, the moon
Ate up her father and the boy
Shuddered as the glowering sky became
All smoke, no flame.
He heard no more the heartsick folks' sedition
Against something—the Market, the gov'ment—
No cadenzas on the shrunken dollar's dispossessions
That day, only, on that foreshortened day.
The startled clamor of unready birds.

After four decades the affluent sun
Again takes momentary shelter.
Now its full face is covered
In living color. The satellite, all systems
GO on schedule, moves, giving
A rare view of the corona as the camera
Swings to shoot the crowd in Mexico
—Indians, bare-eyed, gaping—then invisible
Enzymes power an automated wash.

An Old Photo in an Old Life

A squad of soldiers lies beside a river.
They're in China—see the brimmed gables piled
On the pagoda. The rows of trees are lopped
And the Chinese soldiers have been stopped
In their tracks. Their bodies lie
In bodily postures of the dead,

Arms bound, legs akimbo and askew,
But look how independently their heads
Lie thereabouts, some upright, some of the heads
Tipped on their sides, or standing on their heads.
Mostly, the eyes are open
And their mouths twisted in a sort of smile.

Some seem to be saying or just to have said
Some message in Chinese just as the blade
Nicked the sunlight and the head dropped
Like a sliced cantaloupe to the ground, the cropped
Body twisting from the execution block.
And see, there kneels the executioner

Wiping his scimitar upon a torso's ripped
Sash. At ease, the victors smoke. A gash
Of throats darkens the riverbed. 1900. The Boxer
Rebellion. Everyone there is dead now.
What was it those unbodied mouths were saying?
A million arteries stain the Yellow River.

The Center of Attention

As grit swirls in the wind the word spreads.
On pavements approaching the bridge a crowd
Springs up like mushrooms.
They are hushed at first, intently

Looking. At the top of the pylon
The target of their gaze leans toward them.
The sky sobs
With the sirens of disaster crews

Careening toward the crowd with nets,
Ladders, resuscitation gear, their First
Aid attendants antiseptic in white duck.
The police, strapped into their holsters,

Exert themselves in crowd-control. They can't
Control the situation.
Atop the pylon there's a man who threatens
Violence. He shouts, *I'm gonna jump—*

And from the river of upturned faces
—Construction workers pausing in their construction work,
Shoppers diverted from their shopping,
The idlers relishing this diversion

In the vacuity of their day—arises
A chorus of cries—*Jump!*
Jump! and *No—*
Come down! Come down! Maybe, if he can hear them,

They seem to be saying *Jump down!* The truth is,
The crowd cannot make up its mind.
This is a tough decision. The man beside me
Reaches into his lunchbox and lets him have it,

Jump! before he bites his sandwich,
While next to him a young blonde clutches
Her handbag to her breasts and moans
Don't   Don't   Don't   so very softly

You'd think she was afraid of being heard.
The will of the people is divided.
Up there he hasn't made his mind up either.
He has climbed and climbed on spikes imbedded in
        the pylon

To get where he has arrived at.
Is he sure now that this is where he was going?
He looks down one way into the river.
He looks down the other way into the people.

He seems to be looking for something
Or for somebody in particular.
Is there anyone here who is that person
Or can give him what it is that he needs?

From the back of a firetruck a ladder teeters.
Inching along, up, up up up up, a policeman
Holds on with one hand, sliding it on ahead of him.
In the other, outstretched, a pack of cigarettes.

Soon the man will decide between
The creature comfort of one more smoke
And surcease from being a creature.
Meanwhile the crowd calls *Jump!* and calls *Come down!*

Now, his cassock billowing in the bulges of Death's
        black flag,
A priest creeps up the ladder too.

What will the priest and the policeman together
Persuade the man to do?

He has turned his back to them.
He has turned away from everyone.
His solitariness is nearly complete.
He is alone with his decision.

No one on the ground or halfway into the sky can know
The hugeness of the emptiness that surrounds him.
All of his senses are orphans.
His ribs are cold andirons.

Does he regret his rejection of furtive pills,
Of closet noose or engine idling in closed garage?
A body will plummet through shrieking air,
The audience dumb with horror, the spattered street . . .

The world he has left is as small as toys at his feet.
Where he stands, though nearer the sun, the wind is chill.
He clutches his arms—a caress, or is he trying
Merely to warm himself with his arms?

The people below, their necks are beginning to ache.
They are getting impatient for this diversion
To come to some conclusion. The priest
Inches further narrowly up the ladder.

The center of everybody's attention
For some reason has lit up a butt. He sits down.
He looks down on the people gathered, and sprinkles
Some of his ashes upon them.

Before he is halfway down
The crowd is half-dispersed.

It was his aloneness that clutched them together.
They were spellbound by his despair

And now each rung brings him nearer,
Nearer to their condition
Which is not sufficiently interesting
To detain them from business or idleness either,

Or is too close to a despair
They do not dare
Exhibit before a crowd
Or admit to themselves they share.

Now the police are taking notes
On clipboards, filling the forms.
He looks round as though searching for what he came
            down for.
Traffic flows over the bridge.

The Translators' Party

The great Polish
Emigré towered
Over the American
Poets at the party
For the contributors
Who'd wrestled and wrought
The intractable consonants
Of Mickiewicz
Into a sort
Of approximate English,

Till Auden went over
To Jan Lechon,
Half a foot taller
Than the rest of us scribblers
And would-be reviewers,
Those venerables
For an hour reliving
A continent's culture,
Aperçus in the lilting
Accents heard

In cafés in Warsaw,
Vienna, Kracow . . .
One with the fiction
Of civilized discourse
In his native diction
Still entertainable
In imagination,
The other among
Aliens, aliens
In an alien tongue

For whom the greatness
Of the poet Adam

Mickiewicz can only
Be indirectly
Expounded, like Chopin's
Shown in slide-lectures
To a hall of wearers
Of battery-powered
Audiophones,
For whom his own poems

Cannot be known but
In deaf-and-dumb hand-signs,
No shades of his sounds, his passionate
Rhythms twisted.
His poems are stateless.
Yet it's Lechon's laughter
That I remember,
With one who could summon
A world lost in common
For an hour's reversal

Of an age's disaster
—Never known
To us in our *Times*
A fortnight after
Who read he was found
'Apparently fallen'
From his high window,
That voice
Stilled now
On New York's alien ground.

The Princess Casamassima

After digging in the rubble of the ruined house
For nine days
They've found a *third* corpse—
No fingerprints; no hands.
One leg and the head blown off.
The story in the *Times*
Didn't even tell
The sex of the torso . . .

These were some of the people
Who'd take power to the people
In their own hands.
All their questions have one answer.
Dynamite
Makes non-negotiable demands
For an apocalypse,
In case of survivors.

Once, another world ago,
There was a girl I never dreamed
Would be like them:
She seemed to lack nothing
—Looks, friends, certainly a silver
Spoon had stirred her porringer—
She'd sit scribbling
Notes in the next to the back row,

But I can't remember now
One word she wrote for me.
—Good God,
Was it something *I* said
About Thoreau
Shorted her fuse? Oh,
Such unbalanced, mad
Action is surely extra-curricular—

13

If the discourse of our liberal arts
Which entertains all rival truths as friends
And rival visions reconciles
Could but bring the pleasures of its wholeness
To a mind
Rent by frenzy—
But how conceive what hatred
Of the self, turned inside-out, reviles

The whole great beckoning world, or what desire
Sentenced the soul
To that dark cellar where all life became
So foul
With the pitch of rage,
Rage, rage, rage to set aflame
Father's house—what can assuage
That fire or that misfire?

Power

'My life is a one-billionth part
Of history. I wish I was dead.'

He rips the page from his notebook.
Litter in a rented room.

The neighbors will barely remember
His silence when they said Hello.

They'll not forget his odd smile.
Nobody comes to see him.

When he thinks of his folks he smiles oddly.
'It was broken but was it a home?'

At night, the wet dream. Arising,
He is afraid of women.

In his notebook, 'Power over people!'
His job, scouring pots in a hash-house.

At last he will pick up a girl.
She'll think, Does he ever need love—

But I don't like him at all.
Her Mom will hang up on his phone call.

One day he will fondle a snub-nosed
Pistol deep in his pants.

What is his aim? The TV,
Even bumper stickers remind him

Who has the face and the name
His name and smile will replace.

His trigger will make him bigger.
He will become his victim.

When he steps from his rented room
History is in his hand.

The Feature

Which side were you on in the tong wars?
O the mysterious terror that used to break
Men like chopsticks;
In the lassitudinous fumes of the joss-house, others
Staggered as though from a poisoned fortune cookie . . .

Transfixed, agog through the Saturday matinée
At the heartless machinations of Fu Manchu,
Recalled with dread:
Each detail the fascination of those deep
Bull-sessions in the boys' locker room,

Or, alone in the twisted night, drugged
By dreams of malign foreigners in queues,
Depraved and suffering
Their strange nirvana's torments, their revenges
—No more the marquee beckons with those thrills,

The movie house itself has vanished as
In an opium dream. The feature plays now
Where the kids
Like those who'd queue for hours to watch the action
Make the neighborhood their shooting scene.

Tolerance

Driving through a one-cop town,
I slow down.
I make sure to stop
At the one STOP sign

Because, clamped to the open vent
Beneath the dashboard
(To cool it, not conceal—
It's innocent, *I'm* innocent)

I have a little box.
It holds a little vial
And a shining
Hypodermic needle

—All is antiseptic
And ready.
But how could I convince
A country-town J.P.

Alerted by his T.V.
In the parlor to depravity
In suburb and city
That I'm no hippie

Out to lure some local
Virgin to a cheap motel
For a quick screw and a fix?
Here, look at my forearm—

No scars, no pricks.
Returning last summer
To our empty house, we heard
A sullen simmer

Seethe in the shaggy yard.
Inside our hollow maple
Anger
Pulsed in the hot cells.

A moment later
One got me!—
And as I recalled
My youthful impunity,

How I'd step barefoot
On yellowjackets, how the welt
Raised by the sudden hornet
Shrank with a mudpack on it,

I felt
The murderous venom
Spurt with my pulse.
In five minutes the ankle

Had the girth of an elephant's knuckle.
The knee swelled,
Then the groin
Bloated. Glands exploded under the armpits

And breath came hard through the constricted
Ache in the throat.
'One more sting like that
Could do you in—

Do you hear? You've lost your tolerance,'
Said Dr. Zuckerman jabbing my thigh with
His hypo of redemptive
Adrenalin.

The fields where I once strode
Confidently through the buzzing air
We now keep mowed.
I feel the throb of the testy sun

Around my head.
Hidden in the day's heart
There's a poisoned dart,
The horizon swells with dread.

1957

'Nous battons pour rien.'
—*Germaine Tillion*

Leaves fall,
        cold clouds smear the sky
on a drizzled night
        singing
ricochets across the garden gate
        singing
scuffle and laughter
        jangle at the bell-pull
crowdburst in the kitchen
        by the warm stove laughing
bravado's gang and uproar
        Michèle,
            Jean,
               Jean-Pierre—
the new conscripts' last amicable toot
        in Saint-Appollinaire.
We stuff their can with franc-notes
        for one good long, long night of it,
long to remember
        au Café Hutot
with the red carafes, Marie, Annette,
        to remember far,
far over the sea
        en Algérie.

An Algerian came through Saint-Appollinaire today,
Staggering under his bundle of sleazy rugs.
Little guy with weasel teeth and skin
Like a sunbaked shoe, he looked as though for wine
And meat he'd sucked mulemilk and gnawed shinrind.
Here was Penury's mask. Here Malnutrition
Owned all the bones, and Manumission never

Balmed the hands that Toil made hard as claws.
Could buying his rugs give this Algerian pause
From the oppressions of all his oppressors?
Whose allegories are the wares he brings
To Burgundy? He has no intercessors.
All pity is futile to assuage the wrongs
That made him stunted, weasel-toothed and dour.
He trudged from gate to gate. From halfclosed shutters
The women peered at him, conferred in mutters;
One made a tight-lipped dicker at the door
As though in civil speech she might court danger
From this citizen foe or merely stranger.
Nor did he speak a word out of the mystery
That as he trudged shrouded his misery.

Snow falls,
        grubby along tramlines
The grimed light of winter
        dribbles between walled gardens,
drops in drear courts.
        Girders, in the glum air,
frame hollow squares.
        The sky leaks
through towering sieves.
        No bricks
rise between the girders,
        no walls rise.
The new Cité's a ruin
        unroofed, untenanted.
The riveters are in Constantine
        careful in the scrub grass
bricklayers mind the machinegun
        poised at the village well.
Their untopped wall in Dijon stands

                    backdrop for a legend scrawled
        last night by unknown hands:
                PAX EN ALGERIE

We sit in the springtime garden. A high Mystère
Uncombs its surfy trails across the sky.
Bees are busy. The hivebox, white and square,
Drones and rumbles. Honey and perfume reign.
It's hard to think of the sniper's whiplash whine,
The lurch and fall between the parked machines,
The orange surge, the pall defacing blue
Tracing new epitaphs upon the sky.
The old chateau—our village school—stands high
And green with ivy, an image doubly still,
Stony towers in air, a water-wall
Mirrored in the moat our children cross.
Coffee in the morning sun: the busy chug
Of Monsieur le Facteur's punctual 2-CV
With the world's woes in the papers one day late.
Our concierge runs down the barred iron stairs
Hands on the rail, as eagerly as she dares
To sift what's stuffed in the box in the garden gate
For the envelope her youngest son Michèle
May, or may not, have scrawled—he'd not forget—
From Algiers on a sunbaked parapet.

        Rains fall,
                    and between the tables, trees
        hold back, then shower
                    droplets down. Near home
        at dusk, their wheels
                    stacked in the roadside stall,
        they read of the raid in the papers—

23

a name they know in the papers;
at their table an empty chair.
Summer rainfalls bring
lowings and baas from the barnyards;
in the gutters the children
paddle in puddles,
singing their rain-songs
in the green world
where grain rises
in golden walls
and golden pearls
on the vines bulge
and the showering rain
teems from the branches
as tears fall.

Let them tend the olive groves and vineyards.
Let those whom the muezzin's wailings call together
And they who gather at the matins' toll
Assuage the famished moan, the orphaned cry,
The snap and whine of the whiplash sniper's bullet,
Tinkle and roar in the bombed café, the dry
Rasp as truncheon hits the prisoner's gut—
Pity is futile. None can intercede.
They die for nothing. The flesh of France is shrinking.
In the bitter heat of the citron African sun
Each death lives on, an insatiate cancer cell
Spreading revenge's virus through the whole
Body which for her balm and cure has need
To cauterize and lance the poisonings that seep
From festered heart to numb compassionate head.
We grieve for the grief of friends, grieve for the dead
We scarcely knew.
At the bier, peace falls,
After viaticum.

24

The Sonnet

(*Remembering Louise Bogan*)

The Sonnet, she told the crowd of bearded
    youths, their hands exploring
        rumpled girls,
        is a sacred

vessel: it takes a civilization
    to conceive its shape or know
        its uses. The kids
        stared as though

a Sphinx now spake the riddle of
    a blasted day. And few,
        she said, who would
        be *avant-garde*

consider that the term is drawn
    from tactics in the Prussian
        war, nor think
        when once they've breached

the fortress of a form, then send
    their shock troops yet again
        to breach the form,
        there's no form—

. . . they asked for her opinion of
    'the poetry of Rock.'
        After a drink
        with the professors

she said, This is a bad time,
    bad, for poetry.
        Then with maenad
        gaze upon

the imaged ghost of a comelier day:
I've enjoyed this visit,
            your wife's sheets
            are Irish linen.

The Outwit Song

My only desire was to make myself over
In a poem's truth and delight.
Then the life that I lived became Work-of-the-World
And banished joy from sight.
But I can outwit him.

I wheeled as a bird with an acrobat's wing
And a throat like an angel's oboe.
He turned into spray that poisons the seed
On the weed where the finches sing as they feed,
But I can outwit him.

I made myself be a great beech tree,
All green at the head and the mantle green.
Then just where my shade fell in a cool glade
He bulldozed a hot level parking lot,
But I can outwit him.

I swiftly became a seam of coal,
A million years compressed in my soul.
With eminent domain and shovel and train
He gouged the hill so I'd burn in a mill,
But I can outwit him.

I was the wind that can sigh and sing
And make the world a harp at my will,
He was the ash and the acrid trash
Of the city that chokes on its swill.
But I can outwit him.

I'll remake my shape as a coil of punched tape,
A drudge among drudges that toil.
He'll turn into a new computer.
He'll gobble me whole and print out my soul,
But I can outwit him.

I'll program him to say that I most want to be
The joy and truth of a poem.
He will turn into dull Work-of-the-World
Unmoved by the sight of another's delight,
But I can outwit him.

Print-Out Song

AND his dark secret love
O rose, thou ART sick!
Has found out thy BED

Of CRIMSON joy.
And his DARK secret love
Does thy life DESTROY.

DOES thy life destroy.
That FLIES in the night
Has FOUND out thy bed

HAS found out thy bed
And HIS dark secret love
In the HOWLING storm

That flies IN the night
IN the howling storm
The INVISIBLE worm

Of crimson JOY.
Does thy LIFE destroy.
And his dark secret LOVE

That flies in the NIGHT
O rose, thou art sick!
OF crimson joy

Has found OUT thy bed
O ROSE, thou art sick!
And his dark SECRET love

O rose, thou art SICK!
In the howling STORM
THAT flies in the night

THE invisible worm
That flies in THE night
In THE howling storm

O rose, THOU art sick!
Has found out THY bed
Does THY life destroy.

The invisible WORM

Delusions

If a genius committed his genius
To tunes the time's out of joint with—
Say, a sinfonietta for noseflute
And three trombones;

Or choreographed on cobblestones
Pas de deux; or, beholding the end of an epoch,
This troubadour *would* make the point with
The Great American Epic

In a gab of which he's the sole speaker,
Scored for laughs and for moans
—A performance he won't make a dime with;
Though near perfect, what use to the seeker

Of perfections the joint's out of time with?
His lay he lays down by the mistress,
Heart's Ease, whose embraces he longs for,
His codpiece swelling, hopeless,

Driven daft by the muse he makes songs for.

O Personages

O Personages who move
Among me, why don't you
Guys come on call?
How can I serve the lost
King who, when the Secret
Service infiltrate the Ball Park
And the would-be assassin
Is paralyzed by the beams
Of their binoculars,
Paddles his paper-birch canoe
Where the sun's blood drowns the sea?

Musebaby, what good are you to me
In the dark spirit of the night?
Who needs you more than when the will,
Exhausted, finds dry clay
Where imagination's fountains were—dry clay;
O remorseless Goddess, you
Take your graces somewhere else.
Bleakness is bleak. And you,
Little Boy Blue in the velvet suit
My own Aunt Billie gave me when she came
Home from Vienna,

—You were fullsized, I was only three—
Where's that unquestioning insouciance
With which you bawled *Mine! Mine!*
Seizing all the candles on the birthday cake,
Eating them—Why do you fade
To brown, to tan, to nothing as
The rotogravure fades, leaving
Me alone with this bunch of motives
Scratching their armpits, gesticulating
From the crotches
Of leafless trees?

Vows

I meet him in the spaces
Between the half-familiar places
Where I have been,
It's when I'm struggling toward the door
Of the flooded cellar
Up to my crotch in a cold soup
Of my father's ruined account books
There, like an oyster cracker
Floats my mother's Spode tureen
(The one they sold at auction
When the market was down)—

Then just outside
Before I'm in the trooptrain on the siding
Spending the vivid years
Of adolescence and the war
With dented messkit in hand
Always at the end
Of a frozen chowline
Of unappeased hungers,
He appears—

Listen, kid,
Why do you bug me with your reproachful
Silent gaze—
What have I ever
Done to you but betray you?
To which he says
Nothing.

Listen, I'd forget if I could
Those plans you made
For stanching the blood
Of the soul that spread

Its cry for peace across the unjust sky,
I wouldn't give it a thought if I

Could only not
Remember your vows
To plunge into the heat
Of the heart and fuse
With the passionate Word
All thought,
All art—

Come, let's go together
Into the burning
House with its gaping door.
The windows are all alight
With the color of my deeds,
My omissions.
It's our life that's burning.
Is it ever too late to thrust
Ourselves into the ruins,
Into the tempering flame?

II

Comanches

I read this once: how the Comanche,
Weak after long fasting, felt a slow
Trembling shake the earth—the buffalo!—

And raced his pony barebacked toward the herd.
That morning not a brave in camp could gird
Himself with strength to bend the stout bowstem,

Yet with bursting arms he twangs his arrow
Deep in the bison's heart! Comanches know
The Great Spirit, when it possesses them.

And now the poet, half a savage bound
By the hungers of his tribe, paces his swift
Foray across a desolate hunting-ground

In hopes to run to earth a fleeting creature
And, with the unpremeditated gift
Of spirit, seize imagination's meat.

Brainwaves

When his head has been wired with a hundred electrodes
Pricked under the skin of his scalp and leading
Into the drum of intricate coils
Where brainwaves stimulate motion

In a finger so sensitive that it can trace
The patterns of idiosyncrasy
Which, without his knowing or willing,
Are the actions of his mind,

He is told to lie down on the cot and the current
Begins to flow from his brain through the hidden
Transistors. The needles on dials veer.
The finger makes a design.

The attendant is reading the dials: no more
Input than that from a distant star,
Its energy pulsing for millions of years
To reach the electroscope's cell.

He lies there thinking of nothing, his head
Hurting a little in so many places
He can't tell where. If the current reverses
Direction he'd be in shock,

But the pulsing of twitches and their subsidings
Flows toward squared paper. Is it good
For a man to be made aware that his soul
Is an electric contraption,

The source of his dreams a wavering voltage
From a battery cell—such a piece of work
That the stars in their circuits are driven through space
By an analogue of its plan?

Stone

Ever since the first fires
Cooled and the colors went out of the air

And on my flanks water sizzled and seethed
And collected in warm pools in my pockets

I have not changed. Cold came,
Prying its levers of ice in my veins,

Roots thrust into my pores and split them,
The sun roared overhead streaming

Its heat on my hard glazed skin
Trying each summer all summer

To roast me to ember. Rain
Came again, and again and again

Lacing and creasing my forehead with furrows
And rivers. Later it came as snow

Cracking and brittle, as though
I would turn brittle and crack.

Well, waves have broken me into pieces,
Pounded my pieces against one another—

Some of my flesh is pebbles, sand.
I was here before the arrival of the creatures.

Most of the creatures have come and are gone now
But nothing can change me. Split me apart,

Test me by fire, grind me down—
I'm still what I was, with my heart of stone.

Wind

I keep moving
Because nowhere
Is enough for me—

When I touch one end
Of the prairie
If I could settle down

And call one farm one barn
One square mile of fencing
Home

But there
On the horizon
Are the chimneys—

Smoke drifts
And hemlock boughs
Droop

Like flags
Of countries waiting
For me to possess them.

Fire

Think of me as warmth, as your comfort,
As a few sticks under your pot of soup,
Your friend and faithful
Covenanter, content
To do your bidding
Against chilblains

If you wish, but do not suppose
You shall know me by your works.
If I come to you as a match
Or as candle's tongue,
As a torch
Or cozy ember,

And you, drowsing by my domestic
Glow, should fail to remember
My ravenous burning heart
I'll leap from your larder
Of short
Tidy rations,

I'll seize all your dominions,
Your house and lands will be my garments
Which become me. I'll make this earth
A heavenly body,
Our destiny
A burnt-out star.

Waves

Each wave arises and rolls overtaking its rippling
Froth of saltwhite foam

Trying to leap into the place left there by the comber
That slithered past only a moment before

And flung the bulk of its huge long back in a wild rolling
Surge on the shore—then,

Broken in sheets and
Pools and trickles

Of itself in streams
Of wet and foam

Dribbled back from the alien
Pebbles and seething sand

Toward its home,
The sea,

To arise
In its own resurrection

Trying to become itself again—always
The wind and invisible moon encourage them

To be what they cannot be for long.
O they would stand still with their great green

Shoulders leaning toward the land forever
Flashing their ribbons of bubbly foam on the air

Like pennants of stone

But they are themselves in quest of themselves in motion only
—What is a wave but a gesture of the sea?

Tree

This is a slice of the oldest
Tree the world has known.

When this outside ring grew in the forest
Chainsaws and a tractor brought it down.

When the tree's husk was this narrow ring,
Washington's troops were shivering;

In this ring's year the Tartar horde
Drenched earth with blood of the conquered;

In this year, a black ring—
As a cross was a tree hung;

Gilgamesh journeyed toward the dark
When this ring swelled beneath the bark;

When sap rose here the tree was great
With blossom, with unfallen fruit;

Here, fed by roots that reached far down
To suck milk out of the earth,

These heartwood rings grew firm. Their girth
Braced high boughs, and a spreading crown

Held unchanging stars as leaves;
The tree propped up the heavens

And gods drowsed in its shade
Then, before time was made.

These dates of interest are each marked now
On the cracked disc by a cardboard arrow.

Shrew

Tom Thumb
Of the animal kingdom,

His heart has a quicker beat
Than the clitter of a frightened sandpiper's feet.

His life is a furious passage
Into the future which is today.

Relentless, he tracks his prey.
He would die in a night

Unless he eat
Twelve times his own weight.

His mouth of needles
Makes a cry

—If it could reach us his shrill
Shriek would terrify—

Kill! Kill! Kill!
He harrows the bug,

Grasshopper, grub,
Yet his belly's never full

Nor will he rest unless he hear
The noiseless prowl

And cocked ear
Of the circling owl.

Raven

I was hatched from a bundle of twigs on the blasted branch
Of the last tree at the timberline.

I have plucked the eyes from skulls.
The midden I leave is clean bones.

Who is so old he can unspell my omens?
No one will live long enough to outlast me.

I learned of death from the deaths of the first harsh
        gods and men,
I tell what comfort I find in this world, or any.

Boar

In the mountains behind the chateau where no one could live
In the brambles and only brigands and Maquis would dare
To seek shelter, they are hunting the boar. They are blowing
      their horns
And beating their drums and making

A devilish din as the boarhounds run the scent deeper
Into the enemy forest. He's in a ravine now,
A steep defile, and the hounds are yelling and baying,
Blocking its mouth. The boar's

Hackles arise and a collar of nails bristles,
Protecting his jugular vein. His clumsy bulk
Dances on murderous hooves, in sudden lunges
And the scimitar tusks drip red

And a dog wails as its innards and voice fall
And the pack's baying is shredded by yelps of confusion
And fear. The savage will in this wild boar
With froth on his tushes was his

When a piglet, blind, he rooted for place at the teat.
It will be in the boar even after this hunt is over.
—He lunges again and another hound staggers and sobs
In its own blood. Their ardor

Is chilled by an ancient terror that stays the blood.
If the hunters with trumpets and guns dare step within range
Of those hooves and tusks they will know that single purpose
Of which this boar is steward.

Mackerel

He's one in a million, this slash of silver hurtling
Through the green salt light with his jaws agape.

The rainbows on his belly ripple
Like sunsets over the sea's skin

As he leaps right out of the cove
For a moment trying to breathe the sky.

Let him fall back into the bay.
It is his element. In this cold water

He will act out the rest of his ritual,
Gobbling the herring, dodging the porpoise, the
       osprey's claw,

Moved by the tides and hungers of his kind
From the egg to the egg, to the carrion sea-crabs gnaw.

Dogfish

He lurks and sidles away out of sight. But when you stand
At the rail of a cruiser twenty miles from land
Hauling the inert haddock and sluggish cod

Suddenly one, then two,three,four of the lines pull
Taut in a tangle, go slack and taut again with a caught
Life fighting in jerks and rushes deep under the keel,

Then in a battle of shouts, bent rods and whirring reels
And curses and the pulling of lines in a net of knots
Tied together by a wild shuttle, alive and enraged,

He's gaffed and over the rail, slashing our boots with his tail,
A streak of muscle and will, writhing and gnashing until
The mate hands me the hatchet to hack his head off

—I see that struggle in the mind's slow motion still:
Dogfish, smallest of sharks, who just was the terror
That rocketed through the somnambulant schools

Of weakfish fated for his belly or our chowder,
His head atilt, the underslung jaw of sawblades ripping
White flesh in the deep green dimness.

A stinking gobbet of squid on my hook was
His undoing. Wedged in his ravenous throat
The barbed iron, the invisible cord, relentless.

My arm is unable to stop. I beat the blade
Where the gills writhe with a life of their own and the head
Flops free. His body as long as my arm jerks to a dead stop.

Blood

At a wolf's wild dugs
When the world was young
With eager tongue
Twin brothers tugged,

From foster mother
Drew their nurture.
Her harsh milk ran
Thence in the blood of man,

In the blood of kings
Who contrived the State.
What wolvish lust to head the pack
The memory of that taste brings back.

Egg

Now that Robin Redbreast
Has dropped an egg into her nest,
Round as the horizon, blue
As Heaven is, O lucky Egg,
There's only four or five things that you
Need know how to do:

1. Learn to hack your way out
2. To grow up (and master flying)
3. Finding out where the worms are
4. Copulation, etc., aerial
5. Nest-building skills

That's *it*. Everything else
Is optional, and who cares
For your opinions of your ancestors
Or views about the Great Redbreast
Who roosts at evening in the West?
The Future with its wrinkled brow
Will arrive regardless how
You try to flee, there is no place
But there it will reveal its face.
No more can you escape the dust
Than prove that Night, or Day, is just.
What's the use to weep or rage
Because all Heaven is a cage?
You have your how-to-do-it skills,
So don't peck at the world's ills.

Rats

To rid your barn of rats
You need a watertight
Hogshead two-thirds full
You scatter your cornmeal
On the water
Scattered as though all
The barrel held was meal
And lean a plank against the rim
And then lay down—

This is *important*!

—A wooden chip the size
To keep one rat afloat.
He'll rid your barn of rats
He'll leap into your meal
He'll sink he'll swim then he'll
See the chip
He'll slither aboard and squeal
And another rat beneath your eaves
Will stop
        and listen,

And climb down to that barrel
And walk that plank and smell
The meal and see meal
And one rat
He'll hear that rat squeal
I'll get mine he'll think and he'll
Leap in and sink and swim
He'll scramble on that chip

—Now watch him!—

He'll shove the first rat down
In the water till he'll drown
He'll rid your barn of rats
He'll shiver and he'll squeal
And a rat up on your rafter
Will hear,
        and stop,
                and start
Down the beam
Coming after
With one intent as in a dream—

He'll rid your barn of rats.

Eagles

When things are creatures and the creatures speak
We can lose, for a moment, the desolation
Of our being

Imperfect images of an indifferent god.
If we listen to our fellows then,
If we heed them,

The brotherhood that links the stars in one
Communion with the feathery dust of earth
And with the dead

Is ours. I have seen bald eagles flying,
Heard their cries. Defiant emblems of
An immature

Republic, when they spread their noble wings
They possess the earth that drifts beneath them.
I've learned how

Those savage hunters when they mate are wed
For life. In woods a barbarous man shot one
In the wing.

He fluttered to an island in the river.
After nearly half a year, someone,
Exploring, found

Him crippled in a circle of the bones
Of hen and hare his partner brought to him.
Close above,

She shrieked and plunged to defend her helpless mate.
Eagles, when they mate, mate in the air.
He'll never fly.

His festered wing's cut off, he's in the zoo.
They've set out meat to tranquillize his queen
And catch her too.

Who'll see them caged yet regal still, but thinks
Of eagles swooping, paired in the crystal air
On hurtling wings?

Burning Bush

If a bush were to speak with a tongue of fire
To me, it would be a briar;
The barberry, bearing unreachable droplets of blood,
Or, bristling in winter, rugosas with their red hoard

Of rosehips and a caucus of birds singing.
Come Spring, in a burst at the road's turn,
A snowblossom bank of the prickly hawthorn;
Or drooping in June on their spiny, forbidding stem

Blackberries ripe with the freight of dark juice in them.
If I should listen to a bush in flame
Announce the Unpronounceable Name
And demand requital by a doom

On my seed, compelling more
Than I'd answer for, what no one else would ask,
That voice of fire would blaze in a briar
I cannot grasp.

Shell

I would have left the me that was then
Clinging to a crack in the bark of the tree,

Stiffened in wind, the light translucent,
A brittle shell that had the shape of me;

And down the back a split through which had burst
A new creature, from mean appearance free,

Swaying now where the topmost boughs of the tree sway
At the center of the sound that's at the center of the day.

III

Path

How would I know my own destination?

It is enough for me to set out
To get there
Somehow,

Knowing that in my arrival is my end.

My names are
This Way
Follow Me.

Door

Why should I care
Which way you go through me?

I am responsible only
For dividing the furniture

From the changeful weather,
The past from the future,

The dream from the waker.
Inside, outside,

It's all one to me.
Who passes through one way

May come back the other way.
If what's promised on one side

Is denied on the other,
You work it out then.

Being neutral, I choose
To stay just here.

Window

Is it no more than an eyehole
On the outside scene
Making everything
—The snow, the runaway dog,
The boys brawling and the car
Skidding against the tree—
Content to be contained
Within a reasonable frame?
Or could it be

A casement dividing
A real observer from a view
Of untrammelled possibility,
Its pane connecting
A man in a room in
Steam heat and a battered chair
With his future
Which he could not see
Were it not there?

Perhaps it's the lens that allows
Errant swifts and swallows
In a downward swoop
Of their tumbling flight
To glimpse the man waiting
For the future to happen—
While he's caged in time
They're free to look in,
And its gift is insight.

North

For reasons of their own the red-winged blackbirds
Have gathered in a cloud. They fall like snow.

The skies, the trees, the fields are black with blackbirds.
Black with the pandemonium of their cries.

The only place more desolate than this one
Is this, when the last straggling birds have flown.

East

Always the mysterious
Promise of a new day.

This is the place
Of birth, the distant home

Of the future
God. Until he come

There is no entrance
There. What awaits us we

Can know only
By our deliverance.

South

Here you hoard the green
Hieroglyphs of morning
All the baffled afternoon

West

This is the home of the setting sun
Of the past
Of the long procession
Of the dead.

You can journey toward it forever
Without arriving.
Each of your footsteps enlarges behind you
The lost land you seek.

My Hand

Fetches, carries
With dextrous fingers.

Each knows
Its place

How to grasp   how
To let go

The hand doing
What it's told to

Desiring little
In this life

Hungering only
For your touch.

Yours

I am yours as the summer air at evening is
Possessed by the scent of linden blossoms,

As the snowcap gleams with light
Lent it by the brimming moon.

Without you I'd be an unleafed tree
Blasted in a bleakness with no Spring.

Your love is the weather of my being.
What is an island without the sea?

The Wanderer

This body that has fastened
Itself to the wanderer

Who hastens with mysterious
Balked purposes,

These hands that answer,
This face that turns

At the calling
Of the name

That I am wearing
Like one shoe

—How did I come
In all this gear

Among so few
Clues to where I've come from

Or where
I am to go?

6 A.M.

What What What What What What What What
the gulls scream as they slice the sky in snippets
trailing the herring-boat into the flecked harbor
the truck backing onto the wharf as the traffic pauses
and gasps as the town lies stretched on the rack of its dreams
and stirs and gropes to pull the curtains back as the sun
pours its tinted and tainted light on the early shift
as the echoes break on chimneys and the shards of sound
drift downward calling What and What and What

The Way

Each morning
The past is that much longer,
All our mistakes recorded
On yet another page.
This is the book the burdened heart cannot unlearn.

And the future
With its somber promises
And bright betrayals
Inscrutably beckoning.
We move toward it, the way no briefer than before.

Runner

There's not enough air in the sky for his lungs to gulp
A full draught that would quench the heat in his blood.
His heart is about to pound apart and his legs
Are flogged slaves from a conquered country.
They've trodden the ground till they're numb.

He has run all morning and run while the sun in the heavens
Lurched to the top of its climb and hung, unmoving
All that long noon, spreading the drone of its heat
And all that while his dogged feet
Ran on in the dust, and ran

Past gates that opened and doors that tilted ajar
On quiet rooms and gardens where fountains sighed
And languorous women as the light streamed from their hair
Looked up with secretive smiles that said
'At last you've arrived here,'

Yet still he plods on though behind him his shadow grows
        longer
And the shadows of trees are meshed with their boughs and
        their trunks.
That unending road he treads in a narrow passage
—By night will he know that the path he follows
Is the earth's wheel, spinning and spinning?

Sickness

He becomes the terrain an enemy force
Advanced on, spread out and dug into,

Mounting artillery in his head.
Siege guns all night long.

Blinded by bloodshot, he can't get through
To his own HQ.

They've poisoned his well. His nerves
Have been sabotaged,

His body's a burned-out battlefield, burning.
There's little fight left in him.

He'd put out the white flag if he could
Discover to whom to surrender.

He'd clear out of here if he could
Only hold himself steady

—His back is shaking, his legs
Twitch like a stepped-on spider's.

He is drained, drained white,
White as a midnight frost

And then in a deep sleep it's all over.
Come morning, he's a new man.

Evening

As a corpse
Bleeds
In the presence of its murderers

The scars
Of this grey sky
Burst again.

The wounds
Gush. On our hands,
The stain.

A Dread

It can be practically nothing, the nearly invisible
Whisper of a thought unsaid.
Pulsing, pulsing

At the bland center of a blameless day
It spreads its filaments through the world's
Firm tissues,

Relentless as an infection in the blood
Of one's own child, or a guilt
Time won't assuage.

A Woe

Larger than the sky
That squats upon the vast horizon
There is a woe

Pressing down
On this house of stone.
It thickens in the air of this room,

It is as though
One loved as much—no, more—
Than oneself were trying

To thrust away
With small hands
Stifle of the heavy air

While in the dark
I lie
Pinioned, all my strength

Useless to prize
The weight of heaven
From her eyes.

Thought I Was Dying

Like a bucket
With a hole

I couldn't find
Just felt the seeping

Of my life
As it was leaving

My wife my children
Drifting away

My head empty
My hands my heart

Drained and void
The bed cold

I thought it's hard
To leave my life

With each breath
A little less

In the veins whistling
Till the sun shone black

As though I never
Could come back

The Poem

Arriving at last,

It has stumbled across the harsh
Stones, the black marshes.

True to itself, by what craft
And strength it has, it has come
As a sole survivor returns

From the steep pass.
Carved on memory's staff
The legend is nearly decipherable.
It has lived up to its vows

If it endures
The journey through the dark places
To bear witness,
Casting its message
In a sort of singing.

About the Author

DANIEL HOFFMAN'S earlier books of verse include *Broken Laws, Striking the Stones,* and *An Armada of Thirty Whales.* He is the author also of several critical studies, among them *Poe Poe Poe Poe Poe Poe Poe* (nominated for a National Book Award in 1972) and *Barbarous Knowledge: Myth in the Poetry of Yeats, Graves, and Muir.* He has received grants in poetry from the National Institute of Arts and Letters and from the Ingram Merrill Foundation. Now professor of English at the University of Pennsylvania, he has taught at Columbia University and at Swarthmore College.

In 1973–74 Daniel Hoffman is serving as Consultant in Poetry of the Library of Congress.

"For a number of years and five books of poems Daniel Hoffman has been quietly developing his distinguished art. Now, with *The Center of Attention*, he has found the moment and the kind of subject that bring his forces to focus. This deeply interesting and admirable book is the one his case, up to this time, will have to rest on. And it is a very strong case." —ROBERT PENN WARREN

"Daniel Hoffman's poems are like the ocotillo of the Sonoran Desert. Formal fluted columns all from the same center spreading sinuously outward—formal but snaky—with ranks of little thorns down every regular face. Like ocotillo, they seem dry. But suddenly—any time!—ocotillo bursts out in thousands of tiny green leaves and small red flowers that amaze the heart and transform the desert." —GARY SNYDER

"These distinguished, taut poems range from topical glimpses, taken with the hard eye of irony, at the physical and mental violence with which we have become overgrown, to deeper gnomic probings of the forms of nature for significances beyond those our moment might more shrilly demand. The solemn economy of their language is itself 'a sort of singing' for which we should be most grateful; their angular celebrations are of a free man's praise." —JOHN HOLLANDER